Getting To Know...

Nature's Children

COUGARS

Katherine Grier

PUBLISHER	Joseph R. DeVarennes
PUBLICATION DIRECTOR	Kenneth H. Pearson
MANAGING EDITOR	Valerie Wyatt
SERIES ADVISOR	Merebeth Switzer
SERIES CONSULTANT	Michael Singleton
CONSULTANTS	Ross James
	Kay McKeever
	Dr. Audrey N. Tomera
ADVISORS	Roger Aubin
	Robert Furlonger
	Gaston Lavoie
EDITORIAL SUPERVISOR	Jocelyn Smyth
PRODUCTION MANAGER	Ernest Homewood
PRODUCTION ASSISTANTS	Penelope Moir
	Brock Piper

EDITORS

Katherine Farris   Anne Minguet-Patocka
Sandra Gulland   Sarah Reid
Cristel Kleitsch   Cathy Ripley
Elizabeth MacLeod   Eleanor Tourtel
Pamela Martin   Karin Velcheff

PHOTO EDITORS	Bill Ivy
	Don Markle
DESIGN	Annette Tatchell
CARTOGRAPHER	Jane Davie
PUBLICATION ADMINISTRATION	Kathy Kishimoto
	Monique Lemonnier

ARTISTS

Marianne Collins   Greg Ruhl
Pat Ivy   Mary Theberge

This series is approved and recommended by the Federation of Ontario Naturalists.

Canadian Cataloguing in Publication Data

Grier, Katherine
  Cougars

(Getting to know—nature's children)
Includes index.
ISBN 0-7172-1928-3

1. Pumas—Juvenile literature.
I. Title. II. Series.

QL737.C23G74 1985   j599.74'428   C85-098708-3

Have you ever wondered . . .

Ssssssh! A cougar is coming! It prowls slowly, silently through the deep, dark forest. Suddenly it stops. It lets out a terrifying call that sounds like a human scream. Then, quick as a wink, it vanishes into the night.

Is it any wonder that the cougar has been nicknamed "mountain devil" and "sneak cat"? But you might be surprised to learn that it has also been called "lord of the forest" and the "greatest of wild animals." You would almost think that people were talking about two different animals, wouldn't you?

Just what is the truth about the cougar? Is it a sneak or is it one of nature's nobility? The only way to solve the mystery is to find out the facts.

Puma, panther, painter, wildcat, mountain lion—all these names are or have been used for the same animal: the cougar.

Soft Balls of Fur

As soon as her babies are born, a mother cougar holds each kitten with a huge but gentle paw and licks it clean and dry. Soon the kittens are snuggled up against her soft, furry belly, nursing on her rich milk. When they are full, they will fall asleep by her side, curled up together for warmth.

Before long, the kittens will be spending less time sleeping and more time playing and tussling in between naps. All this is great fun, but it is more than that. Playing helps the kittens build up their muscles and it helps teach them how to pounce and grab hold— valuable lessons for when they grow up.

Playful as a kitten.

All in the Family

The kittens and their mother make up one small family. But cougars are also part of a much larger family that spans the world—the cat family. Even though cougars are not small animals, zoologists place them in the "small" cat branch of this well-known family. Why? Simply because cougars cannot roar! They can only purr and yowl. The "big" cats, such as lions, tigers or jaguars, are just the opposite. They cannot purr—but do they roar! And then there are the cheetahs. They have a branch of the cat family all to themselves. They are the only cats that cannot pull in their claws!

The cougar's closest relatives in North and South America are also small cats. They are the lynx, bobcat and, believe it or not, the everyday ordinary house cat. You may ask "what about the mountain lion or puma"? Don't be fooled! These are just different names for the cougar.

Usually the cougar's lair is a small cave or crevice in the rocks.

Cougar Country

Cougars used to live in many parts of North America. How did the same animal manage to live in such different places as forests, prairies, lowlands, mountains, hot areas and cold? They managed because their needs are simple: all they need is food, such as deer and some smaller animals, a bit of cover from which to hunt and some slight shelter from cold weather.

Cougars could once find those things in all sorts of places. But as towns and farms spread over much of the land, cougar country shrank. Now most cougars in North America live in the mountains of the west.

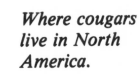

Where cougars live in North America.

Keeping clean.

One Cougar Only!

Today a cougar's home is a piece of mountainland called its territory. Cougar territories are usually quite large compared to most animal territories. They must be large so that the cougar can find enough food.

Once a cougar has found a territory, it guards it carefully by making signs to tell other cougars "I live here." These signs are called scrapes. The cougar makes them by scraping leaves and dirt into heaps and mixing them with its urine or droppings. It also scratches trees in different parts of its territory and sprays them too. When other cougars see and smell one of these scratching posts or a scrape, they usually go the other way rather than risk a fight.

The cougar uses its claws to post "No Trespassing" signs.

Big and Powerful

The cougar is one of the biggest cats in all of North and South America. Only the jaguar is bigger. Not including the tail, an average-sized female is about one and a half metres (5 feet) long and weighs about 40 kilograms (90 pounds). The male is almost twice as large.

The cougar's long, muscled legs give it lots of leaping power. Because its back legs are slightly longer than its front legs, it always looks as if it is heading downhill, even when it is standing on flat ground. If you have ever watched a house cat jump, you will know that most of a cat's jumping power comes from its hind legs. It gathers its hind legs up under it and then springs forward. Thanks to the cougar's long, strong hind legs, it can leap as far as seven metres (23 feet) at one time. That is like jumping across a city street at a single bound!

To keep it balanced as it leaps, the cougar uses its thick, heavy tail as a rudder.

Sneaking up on Dinner

You might expect that a strong animal like the cougar would be a strong runner too. That is not the case. The cougar can run fast, but only for a very short distance. Because it tires quickly, it must rely on stealth to sneak up on its dinner.

How can an animal as big as a cougar avoid being seen as it stalks its prey? The cougar's tawny coloring helps it blend in with its surroundings so that it is difficult to see.

If you look closely you will see that a cougar does not have just one color of fur. It has patches of white and black fur just below its nose that look a bit like butterflies resting on its big upper lip. The back of its ears and the tip of its tail are black too.

If a cougar wants to let another animal know how it feels, it moves its ears and tail. The black markings draw attention to a switching tail or laid-back ears. But if a cougar does not want to be seen, it can keep very still and the darker patches blend in to the natural shadows of its environment.

Opposite page:

On the prowl.

Silent Paws, Sure Claws

The front and hind paw prints of the cougar look much the same because the thumb on the front paw is higher up and does not touch the ground when the animal walks.

Front

Hind

The cougar would not be able to move so quietly and steadily through its territory if it were not for its broad, heavy paws. There are four toes and a thumb on each front foot and four toes on each hind foot. A leathery pad on the bottom of each toe and at the base of each paw muffles the sound of the cougar's footsteps. And the cougar can spread its toes wide to grasp rough ground for extra traction.

On each toe, the cougar has a little pocket that holds a very sharp, curved claw. Each one is about as long as your big toe. When the cougar wants to move silently, it pulls its claws into these pockets. But when it wants to climb a tree or hold its prey, out pop the claws to give the cougar a good grip.

A lofty perch in a tree is an ideal spot to wait for passing game.

Super Sight

Like all animal hunters, the cougar must see its prey before the prey sees it. Very keen eyesight helps the cougar spot animals that are quite far off. And because the cougar pounces from a certain distance, it must know how far to leap. The cougar's eyes are placed in the front of its head and this helps it tell how far away things are.

Deer, the cougar's main prey, have good eyesight too. But they cannot judge distances as well as a cougar can because their eyes are more to the sides of their head. This is very helpful to a deer and other prey animals because it allows them to watch for hunters trying to sneak up from behind. No wonder the cougar must be such a stealthy hunter!

Like many animals, cougars are color blind. They see only in shades of black, white or gray. But they see much better at night than we do and so are excellent night hunters. This is especially important in summer, when the days are hot and most prey animals feed at night.

Opposite page:

If a cougar does not manage to catch its dinner at night, it will hunt on right through the day.

Deer for Dinner

Although the cougar's main food is deer, it hunts other animals too, such as moose, mountain goats, coyotes, bear cubs, porcupines, rabbits, birds and mice. One zoologist even tells of watching a cougar eat a whole meal of grasshoppers!

Ideally, a cougar needs to eat about four kilograms (9 pounds) of meat a day—about as much meat as there is in 36 hamburgers! That works out to one deer every seven to ten days.

It is easy to feel sorry for the cougar's prey, but in fact, the cougar is doing a very important job. In winter especially, it is difficult for a deer herd to find enough leaves, twigs and grass to eat. The cougar kills deer that are old, weak or sick, leaving more food for the strong, healthy deer. If the cougar did not kill the weaker deer, the whole herd would suffer and many might die of starvation.

When hunting, the cougar relies more on its eyes than its nose.

Let the Feast Begin!

Once a cougar has caught its prey, it usually likes to eat in a protected place. Often it will drag its catch to a favorite eating place or even carry it up to the branch of a tree.

When it comes to eating, the cougar is well equipped. It has special scissorlike teeth that cut the food into pieces small enough to swallow. This is important since the cougar does not chew its food first. And to ensure that not a morsel is wasted, the cougar's tongue is covered with short, sharp hooks to clean all the scraps from the bones.

A cougar cannot eat a whole deer in one meal. It hides what is left under leaves, branches or stones. If fresh food is hard to find, it will go back to this stored food many times. But if hunting is easy, it will leave its catch after only one meal. Cougar leftovers are not wasted. Other animals and birds eat anything the cougar leaves behind.

In a dry area such as this, a puddle of water provides a welcome drink.

Cold-Weather Cougars

The cougar does not prepare for winter the way some animals do. It does not gather up supplies of food as the chipmunk does or eat to put on fat and sleep away the winter months like the woodchuck. After all, the cougar's main prey, the deer, stays out all winter, so it can too. To keep warm as it hunts, its coat grows longer and thicker.

Actually the cougar's fur coat is two coats in one. Close to its body is a thick layer of inner fur. This holds in body heat and helps keep out the cold. A second layer of long guard hairs sheds snow and rain.

The cougar does not shed its coat all at once as some animals do. Hairs are lost and grow in all year long. In winter the cougar's coat is at its longest and thickest.

To find food, a cougar may travel up to 40 kilometres (25 miles) in a single day.

Hard Times, Good Times

If a winter is hard on the deer, it will be hard for the cougar too. If there are not enough deer, the cat must hunt smaller animals to survive. They are just as hard to catch as deer, and the cougar must catch more of them to feed itself. And as the snow gets deeper, hunting gets harder because the cougar is heavy and sinks into the snow. Fortunately, cougars do not have to eat every day. In fact, they can go for days without a bite.

Although there are hard times for the cougar, there are good times as well, when prey is easy to find. After hunting, there is little for the cougar to do but keep clean and rest. The big cat licks itself all over and sharpens its claws. Then it stretches out on a favorite rock or drapes itself over the branches of a favorite tree. There the cougar will spend the day dozing or basking in the sun or simply watching the world go by. However, if the cougar is a female, she may also have the busy task of raising a family to take up her days . . . and nights.

Overleaf:
The two-week mating period is the only time you might see two adult cougars together.

Opposite page:
The cougar's unusually long tail sets it apart from the other wild cats of North America.

Courtship Calls

Cougars can mate any time of the year, but more often than not, they mate early in the winter. The female cougar leaves her home territory to look for a mate. She calls as she pads through new territories. Sometimes she meows like a house cat, only louder. And sometimes her voice rises in a scream that can be heard a long way away.

Finally a male cougar hears her calling or smells her scent. He sets out to find her. If another male is following her as well, they may fight to decide which of them will mate. Usually the strongest male wins.

The male and female cougars stay together for only about two weeks. Shortly after they have mated, the female travels back to her own territory to await the arrival of her new family.

Before her young are born, she searches for a den. She might choose a tangle of tree roots or a rocky cave as a nursery. There her kittens will be safe from enemies and bad weather.

Smitten with Kittens

Three months after the adults have mated, the kittens are born. There are usually two to four kittens in a litter—and they are helpless. Their eyes are tightly shut, and they can hardly crawl. But their mother is there to look after them. She tends to each one carefully, licking it clean with her scratchy tongue and then letting it nestle in close to her belly. Soon the babies are nursing vigorously on her warm milk.

The new kittens do not look much like their parents. You might even wonder if they belong in the same family. For one thing, they are tiny. From nose to tail, they would fit between your elbow and your fingertips. And each only weighs about as much as two big bananas!

But size is not the only difference. The kittens' eyes, when they open, are blue instead of greenish-yellow like their parents'! Their tails are stubby, while their parents' tails are long. Their yellowish-brown coats are covered with dark spots, their parents' coats are a solid color.

Opposite page:

These kittens will lose their spots when they are about six months old.

35

Tender Mother

The kittens grow quickly on their mother's rich milk. In two weeks their eyes are open, and soon they are tumbling about. After a while, their mother brings them meat from her own catches. Soon they are eating only meat.

The mother cougar stays with her kittens most of the time. She purrs happily as she watches them play and eat. But if they get too rough-and-tumble, she will separate them, grabbing them by the scruff of the neck.

Meat-eaters such as bears—and even male cougars—will hunt the kittens while they are small—that is, if they get a chance. Before letting the kittens leave the den, their mother checks outside for enemies. She sniffs the air, looks around, and gives a low call to the kittens if it is safe to come out. A special "head for safety!" call warns them of danger.

From time to time the mother has to leave her kittens to hunt. Even then she stays nearby. Any animal that comes too close to the den will have to face a fierce and angry mother.

The Basics

Just like young children everywhere, the cougar kittens must learn how to keep themselves clean and neat and how to fend for themselves. Cleanliness is a must, and sharp claws are essential.

Cougars are very careful to keep their long curved claws well sharpened.

Cougars wash themselves just as housecats do. With their long, rough tongues, they lick all the dust and scraps of food from their fur. And they use a front paw, carefully licked between each wash, to clean their faces and behind their ears.

What does a cougar do when its claws get dull? Sharpen them, of course. When your nails get too long, you clip them off. A cougar's claws grow in layers from the inside out, rather like an onion. When the outside layer grows dull, the cat pulls it off by scratching on a tree. That is what your house cat is doing when she scratches on some bark, or the furniture!

This kitten has just learned it doesn't take much skill to stalk a desert tortoise.

Learning the Ropes

To cougar kittens, part of learning how to fend for themselves is learning how to move quietly. When they first move around, they are always stumbling over their own big feet. But with time and practice, they become as strong and agile as acrobats and as quiet as shadows. They can trot through the woods for hours without making a sound. They can climb trees and move among the branches with ease. They can spring from the ground to a tree branch or leap a small stream. They can even swim—and swim well—if they have to.

This cougar kitten sure thinks it's the "cat's meow"!

Practice Makes Purr-fect

Cougar kittens are not born knowing how to hunt. They begin by playing—chasing their mother's tail, pouncing on stray leaves, springing out at one another.

Slowly their mother trains them in the skills they will need. When she brings home meat, she teaches them to attack it before eating. When they are big enough to leave the den, she shows them how to stalk a rabbit and how to catch a porcupine without getting a pawful of quills.

When they are half-grown, she takes them with her one at a time to hunt deer. They learn to catch animals bigger than they are, to pick out weak animals that will not kick at them with sharp hoofs and to keep trying until they make a catch.

Then they must practice—and it takes a lot of practice to become a good hunter!

Cougars are expert climbers of both mountains and trees.

Life Goes On

When the young cougars are about two years old, their mother suddenly becomes grouchy. She will not share her catches, and when they try to play, she loses her temper and cuffs them with her paw. It is time for the mother cougar to start a new family, and she is letting the young cougars know that it is time for them to begin life on their own.

They are ready. They are almost as big as their mother. They are strong, agile and silent. And, although they will not be expert hunters for some time yet, they can hunt well enough to feed themselves.

And so each young cougar sets out to find a territory for itself. It cannot take just any land it likes. It must find a home range where no other cougar is living or where there is a cougar so old or weak that it can easily be driven away.

There the young cougar will live and hunt alone. In time it will mate and new kittens will be born. Eventually they too will take their place in the world . . . and so life goes on.

Special Words

Den   Animal home.

Guard hairs   Long coarse hairs that make up the outer layer of the cougar's coat.

Litter   Young animals born together.

Mate   To come together to produce young

Nurse   To drink milk from the mother's body.

Paw   The clawed foot of an animal.

Predator   An animal that hunts other animals for food.

Prey   Animal that other animals hunt for food.

Scrapes   Piles of leaves, urine and droppings used to mark the boundaries of a territory.

Territory   Area that an animal or group of animals lives in and often defends from other animals of the same kind.

Zoologist   Scientist who studies animals.

INDEX

Cover Photo: Stephen J. Krasemann (Valan Photos)

Photo Credits: Tim Fitzharris (First Light Associated Photographers), page 4; Stephen J. Krasemann (Valan Photos), pages 7, 8, 11, 12, 20, 22, 25, 26, 33, 34, 37, 38, 41, 44; Tom W. Hall (Miller Services), pages 15, 16, 43; Hälle Flygare (Valan Photos), pages 19, 28; Gerhard Kahrmann (Valan Photos), pages 30-31; Thomas Kitchin (Valan Photos), page 46.

Getting To Know...

Nature's Children

EAGLES

Merebeth Switzer

PUBLISHER	Joseph R. DeVarennes
PUBLICATION DIRECTOR	Kenneth H. Pearson
MANAGING EDITOR	Valerie Wyatt
SERIES ADVISOR	Merebeth Switzer
SERIES CONSULTANT	Michael Singleton
CONSULTANTS	Ross James
	Kay McKeever
	Dr. Audrey N. Tomera
ADVISORS	Roger Aubin
	Robert Furlonger
	Gaston Lavoie
EDITORIAL SUPERVISOR	Jocelyn Smyth
PRODUCTION MANAGER	Ernest Homewood
PRODUCTION ASSISTANTS	Penelope Moir
	Brock Piper

EDITORS

Katherine Farris	Anne Minguet-Patocka
Sandra Gulland	Sarah Reid
Cristel Kleitsch	Cathy Ripley
Elizabeth MacLeod	Eleanor Tourtel
Pamela Martin	Karin Velcheff

PHOTO EDITORS	Bill Ivy
	Don Markle
DESIGN	Annette Tatchell
CARTOGRAPHER	Jane Davie
PUBLICATION ADMINISTRATION	Kathy Kishimoto
	Monique Lemonnier

ARTISTS

Marianne Collins	Greg Ruhl
Pat Ivy	Mary Theberge

This series is approved and recommended by the Federation of Ontario Naturalists.

Canadian Cataloguing in Publication Data

Switzer, Merebeth.
  Eagles

(Getting to know—nature's children)
Includes index.
ISBN 0-7172-1927-5

1. Eagles—Juvenile literature.
I. Title. II. Series.

QL696.F32S97 1985   j598'.916   C85-098711-3

Have you ever wondered . . .

No wonder many people consider the eagle the king of birds. It is one of the biggest and most powerful birds in the world.

People everywhere have linked eagles with power and dignity for generations. The Greek gods were said to take the form of eagles when they visited Earth. Roman, Russian, Austrian and French emperors used the eagle as an emblem of their empire's might. Native People in North America treasured eagle feathers as symbols of strength. And the Bald Eagle is the national bird of the United States.

But like many powerful animals, eagles have been looked on with fear as well as admiration. How do you feel about eagles? Do you think of them as fierce hunters? Or do you see them as beautiful, majestic birds with their own role to play in the natural world?

The Bald Eagle is probably North America's most admired bird.

First Flight

The gawky young eagle peers from the edge of its nest. Its mother waits nearby, her feathers gleaming in the mid-morning sun. For many weeks the chick has demanded constant attention from both parents, but the time has come for it to learn the skills it will need to live on its own.

Learning to fly is a bit like learning to walk. It does not happen with the first try; it takes lots of practice, many bumps and false landings. While the young eagle perches nervously on the nest, its mother calls encouragingly in high-pitched squeaks. In her claws she clutches some meat. Food is very important to the youngster, and it is hungry for the meat. But the mother will not budge. To eat, the young eagle must fly to her.

The chick hops timidly, with wings outstretched, to the very edge of the nest. With a less than graceful tumble it takes the plunge. It is flying!

Eagles Everywhere

Eagles are found on every continent except Antarctica. Some live in desert areas, others live in swamps and jungles, and still others live high in the mountains, along the shores of large lakes and oceans or in forests.

Although there are 59 different kinds of eagles in the world, only two kinds live in North America. These are the Golden Eagle and the Bald Eagle.

The Golden Eagle is a native of Europe, Asia and North America. It lives mainly in the mountainous regions of the west.

Eagle Relatives

The eagle's large curved beak identifies it as a bird of prey.

Just like their very close relatives, the hawks, eagles are known as "birds of prey." Other birds of prey are vultures, owls and giant condors. These birds eat meat and hunt other animals for food.

What do birds of prey have in common? Like all flying birds their bodies are covered by feathers, their bones are hollow and their young hatch from eggs. But they also have several special features that help them hunt.

They have large, strong beaks that are hooked for tearing meat. Their feet are built for grabbing and come equipped with sharp claws called talons. And they all have very powerful wings and flight muscles so that they can catch food on the move and carry it away.

The Bald Eagle has approximately 7000 feathers to keep clean and tidy. That takes a lot of preening!

10

Hawk or Eagle?

At a distance you might get eagles and some kinds of hawks mixed up. Their shapes are similar. But if you could see a hawk and an eagle side by side, you could tell who is who right away. How?

North American eagles are at least twice as big as the largest hawks. An eagle has a body length of 75 to 100 centimetres (30-40 inches) and a wingspan of 180 to 230 centimetres (6-7.5 feet).

Another difference is the size of the eagle's beak. If you look at the profile of an eagle, you will notice that its beak is nearly as long as its head. A hawk's beak might be big, but it is not as big as an eagle's!

Red-tailed Hawk

Bald Eagle

This young Bald Eagle's bill will remain black until it is about three years old, at which time it will turn a beautiful golden corn color.

Light But Strong

Why can't you fly? One of the many reasons is your weight. Like most animals you have solid bones and muscles and are simply too heavy to get off the ground, no matter how hard you flap your arms. But birds are amazingly light for their size, mainly because their bones are hollow. If you were to weigh an eagle and a dog that are the same size, you would find that the eagle weighs much, much less.

But since the eagle often carries its dinner as its flies, it must be strong as well as light. Even its bones must be extra sturdy. Many eagle bones have cross-ribs that reinforce them in much the same way as steel bars reinforce skyscrapers and bridges.

The skeleton of an eagle is very light, weighing just over 270 grams (half a pound).

Feathers for all Functions

Next time you see a feather on the ground, take a close look and see if you can figure out what part of the bird's body it came from. Is it a tail feather? A wing feather? Each type of feather on a bird's body has its own job. Let's take a closer look at an eagle and see how its feathers work.

The eagle's wing feathers help it fly. Some of these flight feathers overlap to form a broad paddle that pushes the air down and back as the eagle flaps. Others can be spread or lifted to help it speed up or slow down.

The eagle's body feathers are smaller. They fit together tightly to streamline the eagle so that it can glide more easily through the air.

Underneath the body feathers are down feathers. These hold in body heat to keep the eagle warm in cold weather. In hot weather, the eagle holds its feathers upright to let heat escape.

Feather Boots

Most eagles have feathers covering all of their bodies except for the beak and legs. But one group of eagles have feathers on their legs too. What do you think this group is called?

Because their furred legs make them look like they are wearing boots they are called— what else?—booted eagles. The Golden Eagle is a member of this group.

The Golden Eagle is more timid and harder to approach than the Bald Eagle.

Feet to Fit the Food

You may not think of toes as being terribly important, but they are crucial to the eagle. Without its grasping toes and sharp talons, the eagle could not grab onto its dinner.

An eagle's talons grip so well that it is in no danger of falling off its perch even when it sleeps.

An eagle's foot has four toes—three towards the front and one at the back. The single back toe can come forward to touch the front toes, much the way your thumb can touch your other fingers. This helps the eagle grasp things.

But although all eagles have four toes and sharp talons, each kind of eagle has slightly different feet, depending on what it hunts. The Bald Eagle, for instance, eats mostly fish. If you have ever tried to hold onto a slippery, squirming fish you know how difficult it is. To give it a better grip, the Bald Eagle's toes are covered with rough bumps that make it harder for a fish to slip through them. The Golden Eagle mostly hunts small animals. Its toes are small but very strong. Once in its grasp, a Golden Eagle's prey is not likely to escape.

Ruler of the Skies

The eagle can glide for long periods of time without having to flap its long, broad wings. How? Like many other large birds, it is an expert at hitchhiking a ride on rising air currents. It glides up on the warm air currents that rise from the ground or makes use of the upward movement of air passing up and over mountains and other land forms.

Using rising air currents, an eagle may soar more than three kilometres (2 miles) above the ground. That is a long way up!

Eagles are not the fastest birds around, but in a dive they can reach speeds of about 160 kilometres (100 miles) an hour. They often dive to snatch food off the ground or from the water, but sometimes they seem to dive and swoop through the air just for the fun of it.

Golden Eagles soar higher and more often than Bald Eagles do.

Old Eagle Eyes

Eagles hunt by day and they use their eyes to zero in on their prey. The eagle's eyes face forward as yours do. Just as you can tell where to reach to pick up a sandwich, the eagle can judge where to pounce to catch its meal. That is important because, unlike your sandwich, the eagle's dinner is often on the move.

An eagle's eyesight is superb. It can see clearly things that would look like a faint blur in the distance to you or that would be too far for you to see at all. Some naturalists believe that an eagle could even see something as small as a rabbit from three kilometres (2 miles) away!

Because the eagle has such sharp eyesight, it can fly high over fields, forests and lakes and watch for any small movements far below without alarming the prey.

The Bald Eagle's intense gaze makes it look more fierce than it really is.

Safety Goggles

Have you ever been crossing a beach or a bare, dry field in a high wind? Did you have to choose between getting your eyes full of sand or dust and finding your way? Envy the eagle. It can close its eyes and still see where it is going!

An eagle's eyes are a very important part of its hunting equipment. Without them, it would starve. To keep its eyes from being injured, the eagle has three protective lids for each eye. Like you, it has ordinary top and bottom eyelids, but it also has a special see-through eyelid that slides across the eye sideways. This eyelid is called a nictitating membrane. It cleans and moistens the eye as it moves across and can be closed to protect it from dust and danger.

Believe it or not, an eagle's eye is larger than yours!

Pellet Puzzles

Like most birds of prey, eagles are not dainty eaters. Rather than carefully picking the flesh from the bone the way you do with a piece of chicken or fish, the eagle swallows every bit—bones, fur, feathers or scales and all.

While eating this way would cause problems for most of us, an eagle's stomach works to sort out the good food from the pieces that are of no value. The parts that cannot be digested are coughed up in the form of neat, hard pellets about the size of small sausages. By studying these pellets scientists can find out what foods the eagle has been eating.

Fish Feast

Eagles usually live alone, flying and hunting by themselves or with their mates. There are times, however, when dozens of eagles will get together. No, they are not being sociable. They are fishing! You might, for example, see groups of Bald Eagles near rivers where salmon are spawning. The salmon are weak and tired, and there is lots of easy food for everyone.

Usually, though, eagles have home territories where they hunt for food and nest. The size of the territory depends on the amount of food available and the supply of good nesting sites.

An experienced fishing party.

Monster Nests

Eagles usually mate for life and they begin their families in the early spring. Normally a pair of eagles will use the same nest for their eggs year after year. So when they build it, they build it to last.

The nests are made of large sticks and small branches that are patiently gathered one by one. After the base is finished, smaller twigs, bark, weeds and leaves are added. Year after year, the nest grows bigger. After it has been in use for a few years it is enormous. One Bald Eagle nest was found to be nearly six metres (20 feet) deep and almost three metres (10 feet) across the top. Even more amazing, it weighed about 2700 kilograms (nearly 6000 pounds). That is heavier than most cars!

Eagles build their nests in safe places, away from hungry egg snatchers. Bald Eagles often choose nest sites in the tops of tall trees, often near water. Golden Eagles often build their nests on ledges in the mountains. They sometimes build several nests in their territory, but only use one at a time.

Opposite page:

An eagle nest could well outlast the original owners. It may then be taken over by a different pair of eagles.

A Small Family

Because baby eagles require a lot of care, the mother lays only one to three eggs. She would be unable to care for a larger family. For 28 to 35 days the mother sits on her eggs keeping them warm until they hatch. This is called brooding. Her mate will stay nearby during this time. He will bring her food and may even share in the brooding. Later, when the babies hatch, it will take a lot of work from both parents to care for their family.

Finding food for himself and his mate keeps this father-to-be pretty busy— and he will be even busier once the babies hatch.

The Hard Work of Hatching

If you could eavesdrop on an eagle nest, you might be in for a surprise. Often, when the babies are ready to hatch, they can be heard chirping inside their eggs.

Like most creatures that hatch from eggs, the eagle chick, or eaglet, has a special "egg tooth" on the tip of its bill. The chick uses this hard toothlike point to pierce through the tough shell of its egg. After the baby hatches, the egg tooth will become loose and fall off.

Hatching is hard work. It may take up to two days for the eaglets to hammer their way out of their eggs. When they finally flop out of the shell, they lie still, exhausted by the effort of hatching. Their downy feathers are still moist from the liquid inside the egg but they dry quickly. Soon the small balls of down are flopping around in the nest.

Eating, chirping and sleeping is all baby eagles can do.

Feeding Time

Now the hard work begins for the eaglets' parents. They soon discover that their small white fluff-balls are all stomach. Their loud chirping calls tell the parents that they want food and they want it now! It always seems to be time for a meal, and for the next ten weeks or so, both parents will be kept busy catching food for themselves and their growing eaglets.

Eagles are gentle parents. They patiently tear off tiny pieces of meat to feed one by one to their chicks. Gradually the pieces get bigger as the eaglets grow bigger.

Young eaglets.

Growing, Growing, Grown

Constant eating helps the eaglets grow quickly. Within 45 days they weigh nearly 40 times what they did at hatching. If a human baby grew at this rate, a seven-week-old would weigh 130 kilograms (nearly 300 pounds)! Baby eagles do not continue to grow at this rate—if they did they would soon weigh too much to fly!

At 10 weeks of age young eagles bravely flap their wings while balancing on the nest's edge.

Leaving Mom and Dad

By three months, the eaglets have shed their fluffly down and grown a new set of feathers more suited for the business of flying. Before their first flight, they practice hopping up and down in the nest and flapping their wings. And they watch their parents take off and land to see how it is done. Then, one day, urged on by their tired parents, they are out of the nest and flying.

By the end of the summer the young eaglets have become skilled hunters. They are ready to go off on their own. Some are nervous about leaving, but their parents drive them off. There is simply not enough food in one territory for parents and "teenagers" too.

After leaving the nest, young eagles remain with their parents for a few weeks while they perfect their hunting and flying skills.

New Clothes

During their first three or four years of life the young Golden and Bald Eagles are both brown and look very much alike. However the Golden Eagle has lighter markings on the underside of its wings and tail.

Like all birds, the young eagles lose their feathers and grow new ones each year. This is called molting. As they mature, the Bald Eagles begin to grow the distinct plumage we know so well. By about four years of age the male and female Bald Eagles have beautiful white feathers on their heads and tails. In this case "bald" does not mean featherless; it means white.

The Golden Eagles also change color as they grow up, although not as much as the Bald Eagles. The golden-brown color remains, but the light parts under the wings and tail darken.

The eagles have now reached the point in their lives where they are ready to start their own families. With luck, they may live to be 20 years old in the wild and raise many hungry, chirping eaglets.

Opposite page:

Don't be fooled, this is not a Golden Eagle. It is a young Bald Eagle.

Special Words

Brood   To sit on eggs to keep them warm as the young develop inside them.

Down   Very soft, fluffy feathers.

Egg tooth   A hard point on the top of an eaglet's bill which it uses to break its way out of its egg.

Eaglet   A baby eagle.

Hatch   To break out of an egg.

Mate   To come together to produce young.

Molt   To lose one set of feathers and grow another to replace them.

Nictitating membrane   A see-through third eyelid that protects and cleans an eagle's eye.

Prey   An animal hunted by another animal for food. A bird that hunts animals for food is often called a bird of prey.

Talons   Claw of an eagle, owl or other bird of prey.

Territory   Area that an animal or group of animals lives in and often defends from other animals of the same kind.

INDEX